Overtipping the Ferryman

ISBN-13978-0615938011

Aldrich Press
24600 Mountain Avenue 35
Hemet, California 92544

Cover art by Jim Haba

For Julianna,
who also lives in a paper house with walls made out of words.

4/30/14

Beth,
Thank you for your friendship
and support since (gulp!) 1986.
We overtip the ferryman every day!

Overtipping the Ferryman

poems by

R. G. Evans

Evans

Aldrich Press

Contents

Checkout Time at the Hotel Insomnia   13

Neither the Seer Nor the Seen   14

Many Feet Going   15

Marsyas   16

Something for Them to Pluck   17

The Body, an Afterthought   18

Jesus Was a Carpenter   19

Experts on Mortality   20

Everything Makes Music When It Burns   21

Woodpecker Is Dead   22

Moon Crystal   23

At Teshik Tash   24

For My Students after the Poetry Reading   25

Cold Soil Road   26

Sometimes Hell Imagines Us   27

Blind Street   28

72   29

Interstice   31

If You Want To Survive   32

Welcome, Guests   33

Women Dressed As Death   34

Death Day Party   36

Bad Oasis   37

Talking Suicide with My Father   38

After They Finish with You   39

Sweetbread   40

The Things That Mother Said   41

More of the Dead than the Living   42

Between the Making and the Ruining   43

These Quiet Nights   44

Morning Storm   45

Every Storm Is the Same Storm   46

The Mute Red of the Female   47

More Life   48

Month without a Moon   49

Mouth to Feed   50

Water Child   51

Flowering Cherry   52

Stealing Apples from the Giant's Garden   53

Upon Reading Snodgrass's *Heart's Needle*   54

Smoke   55

Boozehound   56

Town Drunk   57

River Crossing   58

Dionysus   59

Atonement   60

In the Café at the End of the World   61

To the Flayed Goat Hung in a 9th Street Butcher's Window 62

My Last Door   63

Acknowledgments

Judge's Statement

About the Author

*It is convenient that there be gods, and as it is convenient,
let us believe there are.*

—Ovid

Checkout Time at the Hotel Insomnia

I couldn't sleep last night for the sound
of God's voice praying so loudly to me.

I don't believe in you any more, it said,
but I want you to be there.

I've done so many dreadful things—
now I need a sign.

I lay in the darkness I'd created
and the voice went on,

the litany of demands too much for me to bear.
Soon I slept in spite of myself,

but awoke to silent dawn, the sheets
a tangle of chaos around me,

comforter on the floor,
something scratching, scratching

all around me in the walls.
In a dream, I saw God's neck under my foot,

his body writhing like the worm of Eden,
and I became a flaming sword,

as sure a sign as any that no one gets back in.

Neither the Seer Nor the Seen

Now
and then
we can glimpse
true miracles—
how the body lives
when hope and prayer are gone,
our beautiful weaknesses,
our temporary holiness.
Mortality, our greatest weapon
against the lies that bob nearby like buoys.
The lines we may grab might seem like salvation,
but look at how they cut our grasping hands. Better
just to let the body disappear beneath the foam—
like the holiest of holies, an anchor made of bone.

Many Feet Going

What they don't tell you
is that it's a tightrope walk
and you will be nude, body
all counterweights and pendulums.
They give you a parasol
(too small, a little frayed),
a bright red nose that makes you easy
to track, and a time limit (too short).
If you find the rope is slack,
that's normal. Keep going.
You're young and strong.
Don't be distracted
by the piles of bones below
(Boob! You thought you were
the first?)—but there they are:
waxy winged, chained to rocks,
gnawed through the ribs by raptors.
Your rope has been greased
by the soles of many feet going
one way, all the while
believing they have a choice,
believing they might make it.

Marsyas

I want to make body into sky.
   —Anish Kapoor on his sculpture named for the satyr flayed alive after
      challenging Apollo to a flute contest.

You've done it now, Old Goat-foot.
Wiser to keep to fields and rocks
than to try to make love to the air.

Shepherd-knuckled. Breath that stinks
of country cheese. Did you believe the muse
when she said you were her master?

Another world does exist. It walks beside you
as you scratch your ass on trees, trespass and
traipse around with shit stuck to your hooves.

All animals make noise. Remember that
as the hide peels from your meat,
your last chance to make sounds that matter.

O, pipe-player, tree-dangler, blood-bleeder!
No sky tomorrow will be as clear as this today.
O, goat longing to be man longing to be god!

There's dirt on your knees for a reason.

Something for Them to Pluck

On the eighth day, God discovered
that idle hands are the devil's workshop.
It only took one day of rest
for everything (so to speak) to go to hell.
The archangels weren't so bad,
what with sharpening flaming swords,
polishing trumpets, and all.
But there were hungry gleams
in the eyes of the seraphim,
and more than once He caught
the cherubim whispering to one another,
going suddenly silent and snickering
when he turned his back on them.
So out of the folds of His robes,
God took some harps, a little diversion,
something for them to pluck,
and suddenly, Creation was filled with music.
They felt it in the Garden, a warm breeze
from the sky that made it better, somehow,
to be alive. Toes tapped. Heads bobbed.
The blood inside their veins hummed
and they felt like little gods. The man
held the woman close, pressed his chest
to hers, and did a little box step
through the orchard. They spun and dipped
and hungered more than they had ever known.
How about a little nosh? he whispered in her ear
as the world grew ripe around them
and the music of the spheres played on.

The Body, an Afterthought

for Hal Sirowitz

The story says that first God worked the clay,
      a dirty little doppelganger, and *then* he gave it life—
          but what kind of genius is that?

Surely he had something up his sleeve
      before he hunkered down in the dust
          to shape such punitive bodies as these.

Maybe, like a firefly he'd caught
      by pure dumb luck alone,
          it hovered over his clean, cupped hands—

a will-o-the-wisp, a tempest with no teapot,
      lightning that never dreamed of the bottle
          that could hold it. To lock it up,

he sculpted a cell out of the earth, and just before
      the tides he made could wash the sands away,
          he got down on his knees and blew

his shiny gewgaw up the waiting nostrils of its prison.
      And God saw that this was *good*? Listen—
          is that a tin cup rattling these rib cage bars,

a voice crying, *Can anybody hear me?*
      I swear I can do this forever—
          can anybody hear?

Jesus Was a Carpenter

If he was a framer
whose crossed beams gave the world its form,
or a finish man who drove delicate nails
into the soft pulp of molding and lath,
or a cabinet-maker whose hands' precision
affixed frail feet to boards,

if he favored nails at all,
or dowels or screws or glue—
at the end of the day
one thing only would have mattered:

perfection of a seamless joint,
tenon into mortise,
rafter against joist,
a snug-fit tongue-in-groove.

His hard and callused workman's hands
that knew rough grain so well,
would have known its strengths and flaws
the moment he touched the wood
and dragged it up the hill
to his last site.

Some workmanship transcends utility.
Some function follows form.

Another's tool delivered the blows,
joined iron and tendon, lumber and blood,
the perfect dovetail ligature.

Experts on Mortality

She makes her first announcement—*I awake*—
then springs out of her crib just like a toad.

Something in the trees, some movement,
some violence, makes it hard to forget

today. The chase is on. Daddy Death
rumbles down the stairs right behind his little

skeleton-in-waiting, out the door and into the wind—
she's gone. But no, she's there behind the hemlocks

giggling under branches that creak and groan
like everything alive. She points up in the air

says, *Look! Look!*—and there it is at the end
of her invisible string, the only thing she has,

all that he can give her:
a sky-blue kite in a kite-blue sky.

Everything Makes Music When It Burns

Everything makes music when it burns—
destruction is the rougher side of art
where char and embers harmonize in turns.

Until you live your life within these terms
your sadness may conceal the beauty part:
that everything makes music when it burns.

The aria within our body churns
with smoke and blackened ruins of our hearts
where char and embers harmonize in turns.

We're fuel, and when we carbonize it forms
etudes and scales, and passion's complex charts.
Everything makes music when it burns.

A skilled musician finds he can discern
a symphony where conflagrations start,
where char and embers harmonize in turns,

and even when it's all collapsed and worms
make homes inside the burned out vital parts,
still everything makes music when it burns.
The char and embers harmonize in turns.

Woodpecker Is Dead

Looking for spirits, I found you instead,
    tossed like a coin, tails up.
The dogwood turned its wounds away.

If they saw you fall, the others weren't talking—
    wrens and robins, jays and starlings—
as if singing were enough after all.

Old Brow-Beater, I want to know your secret,
    run my finger through your belly to the other side
where cat or snake might answer me.

I wanted you to be false as Technicolor,
    Old Nose-Thumber, I wanted the only truth
to sound like *ha-ha-ha-HA-ha!*

My trickster, I never wanted anything redder
    than your crown. By your blood I see
something I try to forget, that when we turn—

and we always turn—the old road disappears.
    I wanted forever. You can give me only feathers.
I wanted a body to believe in like a ghost.

Brain-Shaker, you were supposed to be the one.

Moon Crystal

What do you see in the moon tonight, Hsieh Chuang?
Your poem lived thirteen centuries beyond you,

inscribed in quartz even today, illuminated
behind a glass case smeared by countless hands,

very like the hands that carved the crystal hare
who pounds on the moon the elixir of everlasting life.

Tonight I will imagine your eyes see the same as mine,
the tips of fingers stretched toward the moon

or a pane of glass disguised as sky that shields
the hare whose pelt these hands may never stroke.

At Teshik Tash

In Central Asia the skeleton of a Neanderthal child lies with six pairs of ibex horns forming a ring around its head.

And somewhere there are ibex, live ibex grazing.
They nuzzle and rub gland to gland, sweet
grass between their teeth. Some spring,
some run in wild loops, earthbound dust clouds
rising only so high. And somewhere
something larger is waiting, its hunger
matched only by its patience. Older than bone.
Older than horn. It will not lie down
like those who fossilize. And somewhere a child lies
crying wild sounds, its mother joining in,
as close as she will ever come to words
that sound like *mercy*.

For My Students after the Poetry Reading

The poet had read about the virgin birth,
cervix, afterbirth,
gore-slick thighs and all.
She sounded bitter, one girl complains.
The other answers, *Like she's been hurt a lot.*
Feminist. Atheist. Man-hater.
They both agree they didn't like her poems.
I know these girls,
these milky, wheatish girls,
have never sipped a thimble of gall,
never lost the path and crawled back home
through thistle-weed and thorns
or slept the night among the briars.
I want to tell them someday
they will meet the swan, like Leda,
that someday the dark light they refused
to see tonight will burn inside
the way poems burn, the way heaven burns for now.
But we all bow to God from different heights.
When the virgin arched her back
tonight and wept for this to end,
I prayed it would go on, one more mile
to march these bloody feet,
toward such fire, such bitterness, such thirst.

Cold Soil Road

We lived in a house that had no name,
so we called it Charnel House.
We became the envy of Cold Soil Road.

Those busybodies across the street, the Bones,
peeked at our place through parted blinds.
Sid and Nonni Necropolis rerouted their evening

ambles to see our spread at sunset.
Soon, the neighbors named their digs as well:
Abattoir Acres. Knacker's Knoll. Coup-de-grace.

But we were the first. We could feel the resentment.
When the Stillborn kids from down the block
egged our Charnel House, we really lost our cool,

tore down our name, went back to our old ways.
Mr. Ossuary, we see you there hanging
your shingle across the road: Hell's Little Acre.

You can have this first swirl of October.
Me and the Missus can hole up here till Kingdom Come,
nothing between the two of us and you

but curtains.

Sometimes Hell Imagines Us

dwarfed and gnarled hunchbacks—
but often hell reels at the sight

of crisp dinner jackets, David Niven moustaches,
bows from the waist, overtipping the ferryman.

Sometimes hell listens too hard for wails and grinding
teeth—but we are only static, inscrutable music,

voices no face could ever match.
Hell can't wrap its mind around these Noel

Cowards, two-abreast, *After-you-
my-dear-Alphonsing* all the way. Sometimes

hell abhors the way it clings to tradition,
the pomp and circumstantial evidence

of our falls—and sometimes hell wants us
to imagine it as real, all any lover could ask,

the simple respect of knowing when to burn.

Blind Street

It was the year of the frogs
in the city of the Seeing Eye.
Everyone came to Blind Street to see
what could be done. One posed
the basic argument: *They're everywhere.*
Gumming up the sewers. Pissing
all over the coffee shops.
Fist-sized lumps that came
out of nowhere and don't seem to
be going anywhere soon.
Leave them be, one prophet said.
They're here. We're here.
Get used to it. I say gig 'em all,
another said, *every one of*
the fuckers. Stick 'em
and let 'em dry up in the sun.
And the talk went on in Blind Street,
occasional roars of approval and pauses
to clear the dais of frogs.
Folks were born. People died.
Blind Street waited and the Seeing
Eye blinked. Then it was the year
of the tarantulas

72

—To a martyr expecting virgins in the afterlife

You're dead and they know it—
that doesn't make this any easier.

They've sat through endless training
tapes, studied your dossier, your profile,

were encouraged to think (for once)
be proactive, embrace

this shifting paradigm with only you in mind.
But the thing is, they're virgins,

and most of them want nothing more
than to stay that way. In the break room

where a poster of you hangs—eyes aflame
with holy fire, eyes that follow them

no matter where they go—they've met
and blushed behind their veils.

They tell each other you are handsome,
that they are lucky to be the ones for you,

that they could have been the 72 intended
for your brother whom they say has teeth

too small and smells of cabbage and cold coffee.
They've gone back into bright rooms,

your eyes like suns against their backs,
sharpened their pencils, blackened-in scanner sheets

answering *How should you respond*
if he pinches your right breast . . .

cups your cheek with his hand . . .
doesn't touch you at all?—

multiple choices, shiny dark spots
72 abreast, stretched toward the vanishing point.

Interstice

Something coming,
something gone.

I stopped believing in time.
the day my father stepped into my mirror,
held out his hands and shrugged.
I never saw myself again.

Something to put me to sleep.
Something to wake me up.

One morning, the earth split
and crocuses nosed out.
The next, snow so deep
it would have taken days to clear
if days still existed in this grayness.

The phone rings and sometimes someone's there,
sometimes even one I know. Hello, they speak, goodbye.

I'd have my breakfast before bedtime,
my whisky at noon, but for that nagging voice
that stops me saying This is life
and life has rules. I listen, or I don't.

No matter. I still shake hands with shadows.

If You Want To Survive

Don't follow me—-I've already lost my way—-
but I seem to remember it's important to wear white
(even then there are rules: the weather and such, Labor Day).
Forget about winning. We're talking survival. Any bright
ideas about getting ahead, about how you might win, place,
or show might just get you whacked. Now, I don't mind
telling you the world is full of bullshit (one must embrace
one's inner bullshit if one doesn't want to land on one's behind.
I've embraced mine—-I'll be the first to say that bullshit rocks).
But I was trying to help, now wasn't I, trying hard to share
some hard-won wisdom, some pain-forged key to all the locks
on the doors to your survival. Well, I can add that hair
is over-rated. Nothing good ever comes from a surprise.
The moon will sink. The sun will rise.
The safest place to watch them both is buried in your bed.
The best thing you can hope for is a little head
and a larger hat.

Welcome, Guests

Meet them at the door
with shadow eyes
and milk-white pallor.
Withdraw with your candle
out of the draft. Beckon.
Lead them to the pantry
stocked with staples
you never touch yourself.
In silence, watch them eat.
Make them drink the wine.
Lead them up stone stairs
to a room bathed in spiderlight,
where their bed, too short
by a head or by a foot,
looks recklessly comfortable.
Joke about the ancient inn-keeper
who fit his guests to their beds
by lopping off a head or a foot.
Do not laugh as you make the joke.
Back out of their room and bow,
a deferential host they're sure
they will not see again
till morning.

Women Dressed As Death

One liked to pull shadows close around her shoulders like a shawl.
Young, pretty. Not too thin, not too pale. *You can call me
    anytime,*
she'd say. *I'm always here in town.* He treated her kindly as if she
    were the one.

He kissed the one from Georgia, long and open-mouthed.
 Shouldn't flirt,
he knew, but he'd been too long alone, and her smell, my god, her
    smell . . .
Her tongue tasted of lingonberry. She had to go work the third
    shift.

The one in Aruba surprised him. To recognize her at all seemed
    too strange.
The just-there bikini and the tawny, languid tan. They sipped rum
    drinks
and envied the sun its brilliance, the few hours of it they had left
    together.

Brooklyn. Seattle. Santa Fe. At least one in every city. And
    sometimes,
like Los Angeles, they circled him in droves, a chorus of black
    dresses,
whispers and mascara. He touched them all—he couldn't help
    himself.

At home, he spent nights dreaming of the one he'd not yet met.
Would he know her when she found him? Would she smell like
    smoke
and mirrors like the ones who weren't real? His dreams held out
    white fingers

and he took them in his hands. He recognized the place they
    walked as somewhere
he'd once loved. A little creek. A sandy bank. The distant sound
    of trains.
He gave her hand a little squeeze and turned in her direction, the
    way he'd always done.

Death Day Party

A goose just walked over my grave.
  —folk saying used to explain an unexpected shiver or chill

In the Calendar of Insentient Things,
one of my days is marked in red.
I shivered yesterday and wondered
Could it be today?
And one day last October,
I broke out in a sweat and thought
Today . . . it must be today . . .

Like any other holiday,
they'll close the city down,
and I, in state, clown-white, almost
dignified, will finally stop
the X-ing out of days.

There's a box I've left for you to find
in the closet down the hall:
hats and horns, enough for all,
everything you'll need.
And if, in time, you pass the day
without a cake or song,
I'll understand, but for the feast I ask:

be sure, if all these things are overlooked,
the goose that walked across my grave is cooked

Bad Oasis

You never should have come
to this: I've been here all along.
I've been waiting in the wavering air
but not for you. Not for you.
The sands told me you were coming
but I know how sands can lie.
I tossed and turned and called your name
in the dreams I have of drinking,
and when I woke, the wordless sun
assured me I was wrong. But no.
I see the tracks you made, the long dunes
at your back. I see your needful eyes,
your hands empty as canteens, reaching
for me, assuming I'm really here
as I assume you are. This bed
of prickly pear, this feast of jimson weed,
I'll share them since you've come.
You can help me dig the well
I started when I got here. You see:
my hands aren't brutal anymore,
but they've been brutalized.
Run your fingers through my
wounds, and when in time
you have your own,
I'll show you how it feels.

Talking Suicide with My Father

I've thought about it since I was a teenager,
he says when I say lately I've considered it.
Touché, Pere Suicide
and adieu my intended shock-o-rama.
It's hardly silence we sit in then:
in the bedroom, bluegrass on the radio;
in the kitchen, oldies rock n roll;
and in his living room where we sit,
the O's vs. the A's blaring on the tube.
If there's an *off* switch here anywhere
nobody's seen it in years.

After They Finish with You

Did you dream the afterlife
would be such a mess as this?
All that's meant to be
private finally public:
your groin, its gray nest gone,
scrotum, vas, and prostate
knife-slipped one by one.
Latexed hands caress
your colon, climb your spinal cord,
weigh your aged heart
against the standard,
your lungs which hold
what remains of your last breath,
squeezed by strangers into foreign air.
Only your head remains
a mystery till the last
bone is bared, shrouded
by a soaking towel.
Only I know what lies
beneath that dripping mercy,
eighty years of images
that passed through the slate
of your eyes: mountains,
trains and beautiful women,
all you had to share,
drying to dust among the dendrites.
After they finish with you, father,
they'll lift the towel and there
you'll be, just as I've always known you,
and I will snap on the gloves
and dig in.

Sweetbread

In a black iron skillet glistening with grease,
my mother would cook her bag of guts.

The heat would rise
until the pan popped and sizzled,

till liver and gizzard and heart
dead-danced there in the hot melted fat.

Organ smells would fill the house,
a little dark, a little bloody, a little wrong.

No one would touch them but her:
she'd fall into them like a lynx into prey.

In memory of my mother's joy,
I cultivate my inner self:

I grow a sweet and rich and heavy heart,
a liver, festive and fat as foie gras,

a stomach lined with a lifetime of tripe,
a brain uncreased with convoluted thoughts.

When the knacker draws his knife across my neck,
enjoy my harvest as I've enjoyed this growing season.

A nice dry red should complement your feast
with an aperitif (I envy you) to follow.

The Things That Mother Said

If venetian blinds hung crooked,
or dishes lay piled in the sink,
if empty shoes sat strewn around the floor,
mother would say

Place looks like a niggershack.
It wasn't, of course. It was ourshack.
Catholicshack. Polackshack.
Leather-strap-to-the-thighshack. Bigotshack.

Ventriloquist of doom, her voice
still follows me through unkempt rooms,
and I have to bite my wooden tongue
to silence her in the ground

where satin must sag sloppily now
inside her casketshack.

More of the Dead than the Living

The day you realize you know
more of the dead than the living,
it will begin.
They've waited patiently
for you to come around,
to see the world with the oldest eye.
They've lined the edge of your yard
while inside you stoked small fires,
pressed living flesh to living flesh,
rode the tandem tempers of your marriage
just because you had a pulse.
They greeted newcomers without shaking hands
till they ringed the whole gray border of your world.
What you felt on late nights,
whisky and ice chilling your palm appropriately,
that sudden plumb line of night
dropping down your spine,
was the frost their growing roll call raises.
In the morning, mumbled greetings
convinced you that you belong here with the warm,
their waffles and their breakfast books,
but another night will come,
your family will breathe in their beds,
you'll recite all-but-forgotten old names
and wonder where you put your mother's quilt,
almost imagining its weight upon your skin.

Between the Making and the Ruining

—for Michael Rewa

Someone once told me about sonnets,
how they're connected to the breath:
an Italian like the steady rise and fall—
inhale, exhale—of Sophia Loren's bosom,
and the less subtle English like blowing up a balloon
to burst it at the end. But here near the middle of this
American sonnet, where is our breath? Caught
inside our throats, too tight to come or go,
like arteries or freeways not built for so much volume,
or infinite, all prairies and salt flats, one
eternal emptying of the lungs—everywhere . . . everywhere?
This is what happens, see. You start with this
and end up with that. This isn't about you or me
or the weird alchemy of words that can bind us.
Is it?
And here it is so late and too long already,
and I haven't even mentioned love, how things like it
come apart so easily.

These Quiet Nights

Forget the urge. The way you used to feel
is gone, and this is what you have instead:
anxiety. Reminders that the wheel
is turning build black nests inside your head.
Time was, you thought that you could have them all:
the women—ah, the women you adored.
Still time, still time you thought. But protocol
became the only thing you could afford.
Now nights are quiet. Wife and child asleep,
you prowl downstairs, some reading or TV.
You'd drink, but that would only lead to sleep,
and dreams are hard, the way you used to be.
These quiet nights you hear, the saying goes,
a pin drop, a grenade about to blow.

Morning Storm

The air around our bed awakes before we do,
windowlight squeezed too bright along the horizon.
I press closer to your skin, cold front, warm front.
The house rattles to its mortar and boards.
Once when we held each other this way,
your body, a creator forked like lightning,
my body, a destroyer insubstantial as thunder,
we rained and hailed over acres of fertile fields.
This morning, though, the storm's outside.
We ride its rumblings in this haven of sheets,
remembering like a dream when we were made of wind.

Every Storm Is the Same Storm

Storms are short stories, like lives,
rumbling seductions from the purple distance,
bits and pieces of landscape you know
you've seen before, but never like this.
The storm shakes your bones,
soaks you till you swear
you want it to end, never want it to leave—
wind that groaned in your childhood trees,
erotics of wetness, violence and light.
You know that this is all and that this is
enough. One flash and you count to five
before the thunder comes. Then six.
And this is how it ends, this storm,
everything the same as it was, murk
overhead clearing, nothing on the horizon,
the sky in your chest somehow too thin,
too blue to go on.

The Mute Red of the Female

From this upstairs window I've watched
another window in the shed where for days
a brilliant cardinal has crashed

again and again into the antique glass.
He arcs from the waxy leaves of a holly tree
to the cracked ledge of the window and perches

only a moment before battering himself
against the glass, the blackness, bursts of flight,
desperation. A short break in the rain

sends me out to mow the lawn, the pleasure
of domestic destruction roaring in my hands.
For weeks now, we've been trapped

inside by rain—and here, at the edge of the woods
where the grass grows swollen and green,
a patch of red that could be leaf or trash

until I take it in my black-gloved hand
and see it is a wing, splayed as if in flight,
severed where it would have met the body.

The mute red of the female. Again it rains.
Inside at my window I watch redwing blackbirds
dive in and out of alfalfa fields like oracles

and the cardinal comes to his own window to suffer
his twisted image, to break what he can break.

More Life

Whatever fire burns us first, they teach us the word *No,*
but on our own we learn the sweet word *More.*
We cuddle with excess, shun moderation,
its skeletal cousin the scold.
Food comes first and lasts the longest
even when lust crashes through like a lineman.
More cake, more kisses, more chocolate, more you.
In my time, I have wanted more days
to lie in the sand beside the warm Carolina sea.
I've ordered one more drink,
when more was the last thing I should have.
Some years I have wanted more women
than any sane man's life could hold.
And often, when a sun like this one
slips down russet under a dark horizon
I pray *More time,* the biggest *no* of all.
More. Say the word. A kiss into the air.
A gesture of farewell. O life. O now.
O every mortal gift. *More,* we say. O *More.*

Month without a Moon

Any night I like, I can rise instead of the moon
that has forgotten us, not a thought of our sad lot,
and roam the darkened oblongs of the dunes.

Once you said the moon was some pale god
who turned away his face to cause the tides,
and once you said that, I of course believed

that you were mad. Now the ghost crab guides
me to the edge where land is not land, sea not sea,
and all the sky above is one dark dream.

This is the month with no full moon. You
were its prophet, and I am standing on the seam
between belief and what I know is true.

I gave you a diamond. It should have been a pearl.
It should have been a stone to hang above the world.

Mouth to Feed

A feast of nothing, fit for one
insatiable. Inward-turning sun,
we've set a table too high to reach
on a floor too low to stand. Out of stars,
we grind your feed, out of night,
extract dark milk. Rise, eyeless sun,
out of thick and thirsty waters.
We beg you not to burn us as you pass.

Water Child

We give you no name as if
shame were name enough.

We call you by your fate instead,
by your dead-making process: miscarriage.

This is your sister who grieves,
who, flesh-burdened, kissed her love goodbye.

Her desire was a fellow child,
not this pair of liar-parents.

We are father, mother, and daughter.
You are oleander, jasmine, and lilac

in the wind. *Mizuko*, you'd be called
in Japan. *Water child.* Not quite formed,

yet honored, grieved, and recognized.
We'll know you, we believe, if we see you

born to others instead of us. We fathers,
we mothers you have never known

touch the place your absence fills,
wait for your face, your breath, your name.

Flowering Cherry

Fruit has its sweetness to tempt us
to reach the seeds within.

The birds that roost in the mulberry
care nothing for the seeds they spread:

the red fruit's succulence is enough.
And if, as a boy, while burying your face

in the ruby depths of watermelon,
your mother warned you that the seeds

you swallowed would sprout and grow
inside your belly, you learned myth's power

to cling and haunt. Persephone
ate of the pomegranate.

Eden's light was dimmed
by a shared taste of temptation.

But there are no seeds, of course,
in the flowering cherry that bears no fruit

we planted to remind us you were almost here,
unborn one, your neverflesh made myth,

our own unripe forbidden fruit

Stealing Apples from the Giant's Garden

All the children in this story are dead.
Forgive them: they won't know it
until they are your age now or older.

They tell each other tales about the giant,
dare each other to touch his apple trees,
to fill their pockets with the sour fruit

that softens and browns in piles upon the ground,
yellow jackets buzzing, autumn fragrant.
When one takes the dare, he feels the pull of safety

behind him, as if he's harnessed to a great rubber band
stretched to its limit as his fingers grab an apple—
then it's *Hurry! Hurry quick!* out of the garden,

the giant's breath on the back of his neck
(although the giant never chases him,
although there is no giant, and maybe

no trees nor fruit nor garden nor other children
waiting for him to return with his prize).
When they open their fingers, panting,

not one child has ever seen the giant's apple,
a dream so real they can touch it until they wake.
Yet this is what they remember now that they are dead,

when a warm November wind full of orchard
and fruit-falls dares them to believe that they're alive:
one stony apple, wizened as a shrunken head,

its weight true in their hands which seem suddenly
small and pink and real.

Upon Reading Snodgrass's *Heart's Needle*

Ash over all our lives. Archaeology.
I dusted through the book, each poem an artifact,

the voice of terrible consequence. *An only daughter
is the needle of the heart.*

Forty years between his daughter and mine,
each year settling like ash.

All this dust, each night heavier, the very air
impossible to hold up. I want light again,

the man who wrote it shaping breath
from ashes. Finding words to call life

back from the ruin that is our heart.

Smoke

What is smoke? my daughter asks
beside a campfire I can't quite get to flame.

I know it's not a liquid, she says.
Is it a gas? Is it a solid?

Simple. Straightforward. Something
I should know, I'm sure.

I start to say it's what's left
when the wood gives up the ghost,

but then I think of ash—
I always think of ash,

how it's something but nothing,
what's left when something's gone.

There was a woman, then there was ash
her husband and the men she loved

scattered on the beach. The wind
wouldn't let her stay there where she wanted.

My mother, seeding cancer, more ash
than paper dangling from her Lucky Strike.

What is it? my daughter says.
Nothing, I respond.

No, she says, what is smoke? I say
It's what I make instead of fire.

Boozehound

The old boozehound bays at moons
inside his skull where everything is snow,

every day's a bonelit ghost. This is his cage.
This his feed. This the bowl he tips but never

empties. He can't be carrion and his sleep
is filled with stones. Always something dead

to roll in, the scent of something past
but never over. Always something

fleet nearby to set his haunches twitching
jackrabbit fast and gone before the pain.

He bays and begs—but who can put him down
out here where all the dogs go deaf

yelping every time they kick themselves?

Town Drunk

So late, the barstools are falling
off themselves. In the corner,

the Wurlitzer burps and slurs its way
from song to song, forgetting lines.

Exit signs squint bloodshot red
when last call lights groan on.

Cars too dizzy to drive cut swaths
across lawns and playgrounds. Chilly

receptions await them at home—
garage doors that roll away angrily,

unwilling to hold them, no shelter
tonight. Blocks of houses blackout.

Come morning, red gouts of sky
will seep through greasy windows.

Town drunk. Me sober.
Bloody morning, come.

River Crossing

My mouth is a river's mouth,
inward-flowing,
brackish from the salt
of a thousand glasses' rims,
the Ganges afloat with my own dead,
I creep like a glacier,
crooked as the Kickapoo,
remote as the Bloodvein,
through these lips have passed
the Orinoco, Yangtze, and Amazon,
and still the bed lies parched.
I am Styx. I am Lethe,
crossing myself so often
I've forgotten how to die.

Dionysus

In the dream, Dionysus came to me a lizard,
his skin the only thing I ever wanted to touch.
When I grabbed him, his tail snapped off in my hand.

Then he was the rain, and I was dying of thirst.
I lifted my lips, but my mouth filled up with light:
the sun through the rain shone only down on me.

His mother, fair Semele, took me as her lover.
His father, jealous Zeus, revealed himself as lightning.
She went dry as cinders. I went only dry.

Dionysus the sand, and I the broken hourglass.
Dionysus the flame, and I the tinder box.
Dionysus the wine, and I the bottomless cup.

In the morning, I went to Dionysus a god
to find he had become a man. One of us was empty
and the other was the only one who knew.

Atonement

The wind allows us just enough
to breathe. Not sleep. Tonight
no flames come. In this year of grace
the firebreak holds.
This tinder house. This vigil. Dawn.
How many skies like this:
all fire as long as it will burn.

In the Café at the End of the World

The surface of my latte trembles
as if it wants to scream

Something terrible is coming
and of course it is.

That Richtering underfoot is the wrecking ball
smashing one more childhood into dust,

it's the emanations from an IED someone's favorite
uncle just triggered by the side of the road,

it's the wall of water rushing toward the sunken city
where not even dogs or chickens are safe up on the roofs,

it's the bombast of thunder that roars in the dark, saying
Fear? Yes, fear, the next one will be closer still,

it's the footsteps of the giant father in your dreams
burst from your unconscious and coming down the hall.

We huddle under tables for two,
pray to the gods of fair trade,

make our last confessions to baristas
too lost in the ecstasy of macchiato

to absolve even themselves.
I hold my paper cup like a chalice,

begging its runic ripples to help me understand,
but the best it can do is preach in Portuguese

about what happens when the mountain
finally decides to come down.

To the Flayed Goat Hung in a 9ᵗʰ Street Butcher's Window

A time will come when everything you've loved too—
      mouthfuls of sweet timothy, the perfect wire barb

that found the itch on your coarse hide every time,
      the sun on your gray back (small comfort, now)—

will be gone. If I came back in an hour,
      you could be curried, stewed or cut to chops,

but for this moment, you're luckier than the pig next door
      sawed through already from groin to rib.

I carry these things, not offerings,
      just groceries. Quarter pound of chai,

three dollars fifty cents. Broccoli, a dollar a bunch.
      Mangos, avocados, pears, three for a dollar.

I've brought these names, these prices
      to spend a moment with you, gaze upon

your flesh, ruddy as papaya sold
      two for a dollar down this street where

everything is sold with luck, everything has value,
      flesh and fruit and cost and life and time.

My Last Door

after Georgia O'Keeffe

Let it be black on this side only,
        colorless as water on the other.
                When it opens, let the hinges scream.

Let the view be unexpected,
        but let there be a view:
                a place I've loved, a single eye

that doesn't blink as I step in.
        Let me step in with one sure stride.
                Let the back not have a mirror

like some hotel, showing me
        rooms I never want to see again.
                And when it closes, let there be

air so thin I can barely breathe,
        if I choose to breathe,
                if a choice is what I have.

Acknowledgments

Thanks to the following anthologies and journals for first publishing some of the poems in this volume: *After Shocks: The Poetry of Recovery for Life-Shattering Events, Chizine, The Comstock Review, Lips, The Literary Review, MARGIE, Pif, Poems for the Delusional, Rattle, Tiferet, White Pelican Review.*

Thanks to the following without whose inspiration, guidance and support this book would never have been possible: Renee Ashley, Ron Block, Laura Boss, Kevin Carey, Stephen Dunn, Martin Farawell, Maria Mazziotti Gillan, Tim Green, Jim Haba, Mark Hillringhouse, Sandra Kasturi, Kurtis Lamkin, Tom Lombardo, Peter Murphy, Michael Rewa, Liz Rosenberg, Gibbons Ruark, Michele Russo, Christine Salvatore Smith, Hal Sirowitz, J.C. Todd, Marly Youmans, the faculty and MFA students of Fairleigh Dickinson University, and the Geraldine R. Dodge Foundation Poetry Program.

And my parents, who are here though gone.

Judge's Statement

Overtipping the Ferryman, winner of the first Aldrich Press Book Award, 2013. (Judge, Marly Youmans)

While reading for the Aldrich Poetry Award, I tripped and fell into the world of a skeptic obsessed with what he doubts—who takes the symbols and stories of creation and wrests them to his own uses, though God and the skeletons under our skin are never far away, and lend power and support to his poems. The collection by R. G. Evans has the virtues of energy, largeness of subject, strong narrative, and humor that begins with the double meaning of the title, *Overtipping the Ferryman.* He surprises us in story and in metaphor, giving us the child who leaps from her crib like a toad, the man plunging beneath the sea like a bone anchor, the forked lightning of a woman's body, the fusing of plucked music and apple. Wandering in his harsh, lively world, we may desire more hours, more life. But in that realm, spiky thistles and flowers of gall blossom along his path, that "seam between belief and what I know is true."

R.G. Evans

Photo by Mark Hillringhouse

About the Author

R.G. Evans's poems, fiction, and reviews have appeared in *Rattle, The Literary Review, Paterson Literary Review, Lips and Weird Tales,* among other publications. His original music was featured in the documentary film *All That Lies Between Us*. He teaches high school and college English and Creative Writing in southern New Jersey.